Creating a Business and Personal Legacy

Creating a Business and Personal Legacy

J. Mark Munoz

BEP BUSINESS EXPERT PRESS

First published in 2020 by
Business Expert Press, LLC
222 East 46th Street, New York, NY 10017
www.businessexpertpress.com

ISBN-13: 978-1-95253-828-5 (paperback)
ISBN-13: 978-1-95253-829-2 (e-book)

Business Expert Press Business Career Development Collection

Collection ISSN: 2642-2123 (print)
Collection ISSN: 2642-2131 (electronic)

Cover image licensed by Ingram Image, StockPhotoSecrets.com
Cover and interior design by S4Carlisle Publishing Services Private Ltd., Chennai, India

First edition: 2020

10 9 8 7 6 5 4 3 2 1

Printed in the United States of America.

Abstract

Worldwide, there is a growing interest on how to uncover one's true purpose in life and legacy. It is a subject that crosses the minds of everyone regardless of geographic location, gender, age, or occupation. Using fictional, but highly plausible, stories, this short book crystalizes key ideas on how to create a lasting business and personal legacy. With rising cases of depression resulting from personal and career challenges, this book provides perspectives on how to find new happiness and meaning in one's life, while making a relevant and lasting impact.

Keywords

legacy; business; personal development; career development; business impact; career impact; professional growth; professional development; legacy creation; legacy planning

Contents

Prologue

The greatest use of life is to spend it for something that will outlast it.
—William James

What is your legacy? What difference do you feel you have made in this world, for one person or perhaps many? Will you be remembered in 50 years? 100 years? Or more?

These questions do not typically come to mind as we live our daily lives. However, these questions matter because it shapes the way we view ourselves, our goals and aspirations, and even our happiness. This book underscores the importance of thinking about legacy and weaving it into the way we think about our lives and live it.

We all have a goal and purpose in life and the way we accomplish these ties in closely with our legacy. In fact, much of the unhappiness we experience in life is associated with our inability to accomplish our true purpose and establish our legacy.

Human beings have an inherent desire to be kind and good. Instilled in each of us is what I would call *seeds of goodness*. Every so often we hear of random accounts of ordinary people demonstrating remarkable kindness. For instance, in one case, a businessman dressed as Santa Claus handed out $100 bills to passersby. A person paid the layaway plans at a Walmart store. Another paid the utility bills of 36 families about to lose heat during the winter season. Many of these generous acts take place every day, and in many cases these acts are not even talked about and go noticed.

According to Giving USA (2019), Americans gave about $427 billion to various charitable causes in 2018. Charitable giving crosses generational lines. The Blackbaud Institute (2018) noted the extent of giving according to generational groups: GenZ (44 percent), Millennials (51 percent), GenX (55 percent), Baby Boomers (75 percent), and

Matures (78 percent). These numbers suggest that millions of Americans as well as individuals around the world opt to share what they have with others.

People are sharing not only in a financial way but also through volunteerism. Nonprofits Source (2019) indicated that 64 percent of Millennials, 64 percent of GenXers, and 71 percent of Baby Boomers do volunteer work.

There are approximately 1.6 million nonprofit organizations in the United States, and they constitute about 10 percent of the country's workforce (Independent Sector 2019). This includes organizations such as churches, food banks, and cultural centers that serve the needs of a local, national, or international community.

Some organizations are categorized as social enterprises. These are firms that blend profit making goals with a socially driven agenda supporting the needs of the community, environment, and its stakeholder network. A Deloitte (2018) report underscores the growing importance of social capital in defining an organization's purpose, its relationships, and its future success.

There are intriguing questions to all these: *Why are people giving away their time and money? What prompts them to do so? Why are organizations being set up solely to help others? Why is there an emerging trend among companies worldwide to boost their social capital and engagement with the community?*

I would argue that the *seeds of goodness* within all of us drive some of these actions. We are all motivated to be loved, respected, and thought of in a positive way. At the end of our lives, we would like our friends and loved ones to say that we had a meaningful life and that we have made a difference in this world.

I'd like to introduce the notion of **Memorial Capacity** (MC) or the ability of an individual to continue to be remembered in future generations. Who do you think are examples of individuals who have Very High Memorial Capacity? Some might pick spiritual personalities such as Jesus Christ or Buddha. Others might pick accomplished politicians or heads of state such as President Abraham Lincoln. Others might pick highly intelligent people like Albert Einstein or Isaac Newton. Some might pick talented artists such as Leonardo da Vinci and Pablo Picasso or composers such as Ludwig van Beethoven, Wolfgang Amadeus Mozart, and Johann Sebastian Bach.

The reality is that some individuals have a much higher MC than others.

In my view, there are variations with regard to MC.

Level 1: Extraordinary Memorial Capacity (EMC). Some individuals have passed on a legacy that extends to over a thousand years. A classic example would be Jesus Christ, Prophet Muhammad, Siddhartha Gautama or Buddha. These individuals founded a religion that continues to be practiced worldwide to this day.

Level 2: Very High Memorial Capacity (VHMC). There are people who are remembered for their accomplishments for a period exceeding 500 years. For example, Queen Elizabeth I, William Shakespeare, and Rembrandt van Rijn. Through their remarkable talent and achievements, they are remembered even in the present time.

Level 3: High Memorial Capacity (HMC). Due to their remarkable achievements and talent, there are people that are remembered for a period of over 100 years. There are several in this category including musicians, entertainers, athletes, authors, businessmen, philanthropists, and inventors among others. For example, Wilhelm Friedemann Bach.

Level 4: Moderate Memorial Capacity (MMC). There are special and well-loved personalities that continue to be in people's minds for over 50 years after they have passed. Many are included in this category including professionals, entrepreneurs, and family members. One example would be one's grandparent.

Level 5: Low Memorial Capacity (LMC). These individuals are soon forgotten shortly after their death. The majority are in this category. These individuals are vaguely remembered not because of their lack of talent, ability, or effort but because the impact they have made living their lives was rather minimal.

Now the hard question—*Which category will you likely be in? Is this fine with you, or would you prefer to do better? How would you really like to live your life to optimize your abilities and make a significant and lasting impact?*

It is estimated that about 151,600 people die every day. How many of them will be remembered past 50 years?

The objective of this book is to rethink the notion of legacy and help readers worldwide understand how to live more meaningful lives and optimize one's MC.

When starting to think about one's memorial footprint, it is helpful to consider the key dimensions that shape a legacy. There are at least five noteworthy attributes of legacy:

Depth. *What is your depth of impact?* For instance, a professor who has mentored a student or a physician who has saved someone's life would have a deep impact on a person's life.

Scale. *How many lives have you touched?* An author who wrote a best-selling self-help book that transformed many lives or a politician that initiated a bill that provided better health care to the citizenry has made an impact on lives on a grand scale.

Scope. *How many segments in society were you able to transform?* A famous actress who has made dramatic contributions in the entertainment industry might also have led the effort to fight world hunger and have been a major donor in the art community. In this case, the scope of her impact is wide.

Time. *When did you start making an impact on society?* If there was such a thing as a legacy balance sheet based on one's impact on society, there is a good chance that those who started engaging in socially driven pursuits earlier in life could have made a bigger difference than those who decided to act during the last days of their lives.

Inertia. *How much energy did you expend in trying to make a difference?* It is fairly obvious that a person who has put in a lot of energy in social change would have a greater memorial trajectory and velocity as compared to one who has put in a minimal or no effort.

These dimensions highlight the fact that there are variations in which people pursue social impact and create their legacy. The choices one makes eventually determines one's MC.

As human beings in a global village, we are endowed with different talents, abilities, and resources. *If we want to enrich our memorial capacity and optimize our legacy in our society, what can we do? What were the success formulas of Jesus Christ or William Shakespeare or Wilhelm Friedemann Bach? Is there something we can learn from truly memorable people?*

In my assessment, there are several legacy pathways. Here are eight powerful examples:

Financial. A case in point would be a billionaire who successfully created a business empire. After building much wealth, he decides to give most of it to charity. Think Bill Gates.

Social. One example would be an entrepreneur who revolutionized the way people socialize through the web worldwide. Think Mark Zuckerberg.

Political. A President of a country may have made defining decisions that changed the course of a nation. Think Abraham Lincoln and Margaret Thatcher.

Intellectual. An inventor may have created a practical product that helped industrialize the world. Think Thomas Edison.

Spiritual. A person may have initiated a revolutionary spiritual movement. Think Martin Luther and Mother Theresa.

Cultural. An activist may have pursued nonviolent civil disobedience that inspired civil rights movements around the world. Think Mahatma Gandhi.

Physical. A competitive swimmer may have elevated the sport of competitive swimming by winning a total of 28 gold medals and eventually becoming the world's most decorated Olympian. Think Michael Phelps.

Historical. An explorer and navigator may have pioneered European expeditions in the Caribbean, Central America, and South America initiating colonization of the Americas. Think Christopher Columbus.

These examples are amazing accomplishments of men and women. They all have high MCs as a result of their skills and actions.

However, simple people, with far less abilities, are in a position to enhance and enrich their MC. Strategizing through the five dimensions of legacy—depth, scale, scope, time, and inertia, we can all make an impact in the world in our own way.

This book showcases eight fictional, but plausible, stories of how contemporary individuals can create a lasting legacy. These stories offer important lessons that can inspire you to use whatever talent, abilities, and resources you have to make the world a better place. A summary of the lessons learned will be highlighted and discussed and the concept of a Strategic Legacy Plan (SLP) will be introduced. A conclusion chapter sums up the key lessons for a successful legacy creation.

We are in this world not to merely exist, but to make an impact in our own way and leave behind a meaningful legacy.

References

Blackbaud Institute. 2018. "The Next Generation of American Giving." https://cdn.fedweb.org/fed-115/2/2018-Next-Generation-of-Giving .pdf.

Deloitte. 2018. "The Rise of the Social Enterprise. 2018 Deloitte Global Human Capital Trends." https://www2.deloitte.com/content/dam/ insights/us/articles/HCTrends2018/2018-HCtrends_Rise-of-the-social-enterprise.pdf.

Giving USA. 2019. "Americans Gave $427.71 Billion to Charity in 2018 Amid Complex Year for Charity Giving." https://givingusa .org/giving-usa-2019-americans-gave-427-71-billion-to-charity-in-2018-amid-complex-year-for-charitable-giving/.

Independent Sector. 2019. "The Charitable Sector." https://independent-sector.org/about/the-charitable-sector/.

Nonprofits Source. 2019. "The Ultimate List of Charitable Giving Statistics for 2018." https://nonprofitssource.com/online-giving-statistics/.

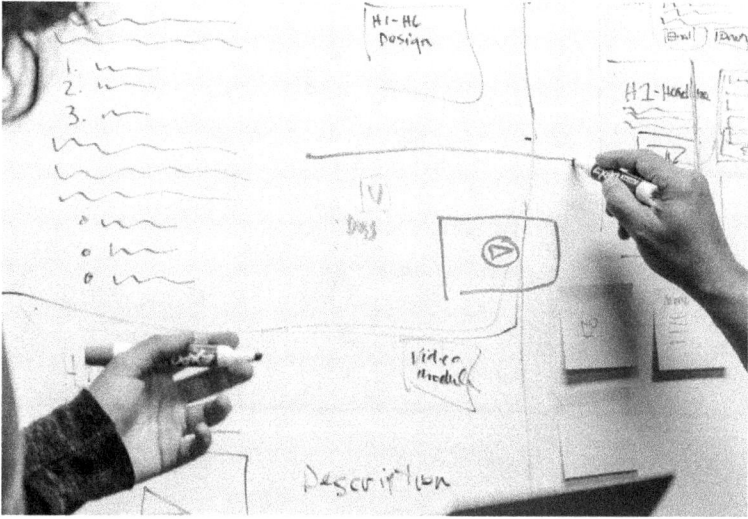

Art courtesy of Allison Brannon

Acknowledgments

In one's lifetime, there are times when a pursued endeavor feels like it is driven by a higher power. Progress takes place seamlessly, and obstacles seem to miraculously disappear. This is one such endeavor. Rob Zwettler, Vilma Barr, and Allison Brannon seemed like angels who helped advance this book project. My family and friends have been a constant source of inspiration. I am most grateful for all the love and support I received. I hope readers will be touched by the featured stories and will strive to accomplish meaningful lives that make an impact in our global community. This book is an attempt to encourage readers to think about how they would want to be remembered in their lifetime. In a small and very humble way—this book is my legacy.

CHAPTER 1

Jack Wilson:
Financial Legacy

Every person has a legacy. You may not know what your impact is, and it may not be something that you can write on your tombstone, but every person has an impact on this world.

—Dara Horn

Jack Wilson wiped the sweat in his brow as the scorching heat of Australian outback practically zapped all his energy.

He stared intently at the vast expanse of his property. How long have I been doing this? he wondered. Was it 18 years or 20? It doesn't matter, he deliberated; all his hard work paid off and he was a millionaire many times over. No—not just a millionaire, a billionaire. The enormous amount of helium uncovered in his property had a valuation of over $20 billion. As a major stockholder in his company, he now had more than enough money to last a lifetime. Actually, he'd be good for several lifetimes. Now what?

His personal assistant Jeff Brown interrupted his train of thought.

"Jack, you need to sign these forms," he said matter-of-factly. "Billing invoices."

Jack nodded and quietly signed the forms.

"Are you okay?" Jeff asked.

"Just thinking," Jack muttered.

"About what?" Jeff inquired curiously. He made it a point to be on top of everything and efficiently cater to whatever Jack needed.

"What's all these for?"

"What do you mean?" Jeff continued, totally confused with Jack's question.

"What's all these wealth for?" Jack pondered.

Jeff stared at his boss puzzled. He managed a response to what seemed like a philosophical question.

"Well, Jack this wealth keeps the company afloat. It also creates jobs, helps the economy, and our government through taxes."

Jack smiled, amused. His assistant's practical view of business and life is what endeared him. Jack has lost count of the times Jeff's pragmatism have prevented him from making business blunders. They work well together. Jack was bold, ambitious, and a big thinker. Jeff was calm, collected, and provides keen attention to detail.

"I'm at the stage in my life where I need more in life than wealth." Jack said. He was thinking out load. The thought surprised him.

"What else would you like to do, Jack," Jeff countered.

"I haven't given it much thought. But I want to do something meaningful."

"Isn't our company meaningful enough? We've built one of the largest companies in Australia!" Jeff looked at him curiously.

"At times, I feel an empty void inside of me. It's as if something is missing." Jack said, walking toward the worksite shed.

Jeff followed him. "Well, what is it that you want to do? What would help add meaning to the company? I can ask Beth Morris of Corporate Affairs to drum up a new community program initiative."

Jack shook his head, "No, this isn't about the company anymore. This is personal. I'm getting old. I'd like to step down as CEO, stay on as Chairman, and spend the rest of my days doing philanthropy or something. I haven't figured out exactly what yet."

Jeff was dumbfounded but kept his composure. It was the first time he heard his boss speak this way. For as long as he has known him, he was always driven by wealth and achievement—nothing else. His two divorces and weak relationships with his children ended up as the spoils of his quest. This was indeed a surprise. The fact that Jack said this during the highest point of his career, and at the time when his business empire was doing extremely well was completely out of character. Over the years, Jeff learned when to hold back and let his boss do the talking. He took pride in the fact that he was also Jack's confidante, friend, and advisor. He knew him well enough to know when to intervene and when to step back. At this time, his instincts told him to step back and merely listen.

There was a long silence as Jack started to gather his belongings.

Jeff managed to speak, "Well, I'm here for you. Let me know if you need my help on anything."

Jack nodded and said, "Well, there's actually something I'd like you to do. I'd like you to do some research on the poorest island communities around the world and see what sort of help they need to improve their lives."

Jeff was curious, "Any particular community of interest?"

"All of them. Actually, start off with the "*badjaos*" in the Malaysia, Philippines, and Indonesia." Jack paused and was suddenly pensive.

Jeff started to take notes.

Jack continued, "I never told you this, but when I was about ten years old my family and I vacationed in Borneo. On a fishing trip with my dad, I slipped and fell off the boat. I nearly drowned and a *badjao* family nearby jumped in and saved me. I wouldn't be here today if those sea gypsies did not step in to help. I've been reading about that maritime ethnic group over the years, but never lifted a finger to help. This time, I want to make a difference. I want to use my wealth and influence to improve their plight. Actually, I want to help not just for the *badjaos* in Southeast Asia but all struggling island communities around the world.

Jeff continued taking notes and said, "I'll get working on it straight away. This is a personal initiative right? Something like a Jack Wilson Foundation?"

Jack smiled, "Yes." He has always been impressed by Jeff's efficiency and work tempo. He does not only do things very well, he does things fast.

Jeff smiled back, "Consider it done. Happy to help you make this a reality. How much funds should I block off for this endeavor?"

Without hesitation Jack said, "A billion dollars."

Legacy Lesson 1: Leverage your financial resources to make an impact.

Art courtesy of Allison Brannon

CHAPTER 2

Aya Rahal: Social Legacy

Carve your name on hearts, not tombstones. A legacy is etched into the minds of others and the stories they share about you.

—Shannon Adler

Aya Rahal kissed her girlfriend Loulia Bahar passionately. She was ecstatic that they were able to spend the night together. Her joy was short-lived. Immediately, it crossed her mind that it could be months before they could spend time like this again.

Aya was a widow, so there were no hitches on her end. Loulia, on the other hand, was engaged. She had to lie to her fiancée about this trip and claimed she had to address a family emergency. Like other Middle Eastern lesbians, they had to keep their affair very secret. Aside from themselves, nobody else knew.

On many occasions, Aya hated herself. Why did she have to turn out this way? She wondered. Why can't she simply be like other women? The passion she and Loulia felt for each other was insatiable. They longed for each other's company every day, every hour, and every minute.

What suddenly crossed her mind brought immediate fear. She wondered whether her mobile phone may be traced. If someone traced her calls, they'd be suspicious about the volume of calls she and Loulia made to each other.

The past 6 months completely transformed her life. From being a tech specialist clerk in a Middle Eastern bank, she had evolved into one of the most influential gay activist leaders in the Middle East and Africa. She did it all through social media and a transcripted lesbian, gay, bisexual, transgender, and questioning (or queer) (LGBTQ) matching service through a website and app. She initiated the effort in a desperate move to find a partner in this impossible environment. Little did she know that in just a few months there would be close to a million subscribers worldwide. Had it not been through the assistance of her cousin Ahmed, she could not have managed the overwhelming subscription and community support. The website crashed more than a dozen times in the first month of operation.

She still recalls the conversation she had with Ahmed one night in her home.

It was after a family reunion dinner and when all the guests left, she pulled Ahmed to one corner.

"Ahmed, I need to talk to you. Please come with me."

They sat in a couch in quiet corner room in her house. It was her home office, library, and sanctuary. This was the place where it all began. The exact spot where she created the website and app that started the gay rights movement in the Middle East and Africa.

Her heart was beating so fast that it made her dizzy. She noticed that her hands were literally shaking. Ahmed was her cousin and one of her closest friends, yet there are many things she couldn't tell him. But given the technological problems she was experiencing in the website and the app, Ahmed was her best bet. He was a master web designer and entrepreneur. He had studied in Europe and can view the world in many lenses. Yet, from their upbringing, she wasn't sure how he would react to what he was about to tell him. She had no choice.

Her voice shook when she said, "Ahmed... I... I am a lesbian."

Tears rolled down her eyes as Ahmed looked at her sadly.

"I'm sorry..." he said in a meek voice, "I mean, I understand...but this must be very difficult."

"It is...," Aya said in a trailing voice.

There was complete silence. It was as if the stillness of the night from outside the room crept quietly inside and surrounded them.

Ahmed stammered saying, "Why... I mean... Why are you telling me this? Why now?"

Aya regained her composure. Some people described her as tough. In the heat of adversity, she rises like a wounded warrior battling for life. In this case, she had no choice. She had to be strong. If this technical problem won't be resolved, people will complain and investigate. She was uncertain about her web security as well. If someone hacks the site, someone would be able to identify her. It would be like coming out to the whole world! And from a Middle Eastern country of all places! Her entire country will crucify her. Ahmed's expertise in web security is her sole salvation. There was no other option.

"Have you heard about the website and app "Yuzhir" or come out?" she asked tentatively.

"Yes, who hasn't? The site is growing to be immensely popular. Did you get listed in the site?"

Aya shook her head, "No... not just that. I started it. I built the entire program."

Ahmed looked at her astoundingly. "You?..."

"Yes" Aya said, "I never expected it to get this crazy."

Ahmed looked worried, "My cousin, you could be in grave danger. It might be best for you to leave the country right away. If you wish to continue the site, run it from America or in a clandestine location somewhere in Europe."

"I can. But, I have bigger problems at the moment. The website has crashed several times and I don't know how to fix it. Moreover, I think the web security has been compromised. I need help fast. Can you please help me?"

Ahmed looked at her intently, "Of course, my dear cousin. Show me the program."

That conversation took place several months back. A lot has happened since then. Ahmed became more involved in the enterprise. In fact, he agreed to become co-founder. They set up an office in a discreet location in the United States. They upgraded the server capacity in order to handle millions of users and avoid instances of website crashing. In addition, they invested heavily in security and privacy protocols. Ahmed added his entrepreneurial flair by pursuing several revenue streams. They were able to attract several major advertisers. The majority of users opted to pay a fee rather than just use the free service. The enterprise soon started to be very profitable and sustainable. In just a few months, Yuzhir became not only the fastest growing website in the Middle East but also the most influential force in the gay rights movement in the Middle East and Africa. While operating anonymously, it was able to push for policy reform as well as fair treatment for the LGBTQ community in business, academia, and government organizations.

Aya stared at Loulia as they lay together in bed. She gave her a passionate kiss. Perhaps, she thought, they could be together after all. With the world changing in the strange ways it does, maybe there's hope for them.

Legacy Lesson 2: Use social capital to make a dramatic change.

Art courtesy of Allison Brannon

CHAPTER 3

Philip Gomez: Political Legacy

I feel that my father's greatest legacy was the people he inspired to get involved in public service and their communities, to join the Peace Corps, to go into space. And really that generation transformed the country in civil rights, social justice, the economy and everything.
—Caroline Kennedy

Philip Gomez glared at his fellow congressman Augusto Bonifacio, who was seated across him. Part of him literally wanted to wring his neck.

He cursed in the local language and banged his hand on the table, "You can't do that! You'll be putting the lives of hundreds of men, women, and children at risk."

Both congressmen represent a Southern region of the Philippines. The areas in their jurisdiction have experienced a rapid inflow of refugees from an Asian country that has experienced an extreme natural calamity and political turmoil. With nowhere else to go, hundreds of thousands of refugees embarked in makeshift canoes and made their way to the Philippine shores.

The two congressmen were at odds on what to do. Philip Gomez wanted to take them in and send them to an unused large tract of land by the mountains and help them rebuild their lives and start a community. Augusto Bonifacio wanted to pile all the refugees up in navy ships and send them back to their countries.

Both men were passionate about their opinion on the right course of action and had been engaged in a yelling match. The meeting room was starting to look like a circus. The congressmen's equally passionate constituents were about ready to start a brawl. Media representatives were recording the dramatic exchange on live television. The phones were constantly ringing at the President's office, international media, and other international organizations were trying to reach the men.

Both men belonged to the same political party and were close to the President. The politically astute President left the decision making to them suggesting that they resolve their differences and come up with a viable solution. With the presidential elections not too far away, the President figured it was wise not to get embroiled in this politically charged event and preferred to have the congressmen resolve the issue.

Philip decided to try an emotional appeal to convince his colleague, "Look, Augusto. Think of it this way. If a major calamity happened to the Philippines, and we all had to leave, and you and your family fled in a canoe in an effort to survive, wouldn't you want a country to take you in?"

Augusto shook his head, "You don't get the point, Philip. It's not that I don't want to help. We don't have resources to help. We are not a rich country. Millions are already suffering in our own country. We have more people to take care of?"

"But, where are this people to go? They have no other option. We're looking at a life and death situation here. If we don't take them in, many of them will die. Do you want to take part in a genocide?" Philip argued passionately.

Augusto stood his ground, "Our country should come first, Philip. We were elected by our constituents to protect their interest. The needs of our people should be paramount."

Philip disagreed, "This is no longer an issue about our constituents or our country; this is an international matter. We are global citizens. Besides, the entire international community offered to help. It's no longer an issue of resources. We have received a pledge of over a billion dollars from foreign countries to help establish a living community for these refugees here."

"A billion dollars is hardly enough. Besides, it's not just about the money. It's the hassle of it all. It will derail us from our economic development plans." Augusto countered in an exasperated manner.

"Is saving lives a hassle for you, Augusto?" Philip screamed.

Loud yelling erupted around the room while the media lambasted the duo with questions.

Philip ignored the noise and continued, "The living community can be our new economic platform. Many of these refugees are educated, some even have money of their own. They can offer professional services to our people, start businesses, generate jobs, and pay taxes. They won't weaken the economy. They will strengthen it. The living community will have a buzzing economic ecosystem. It will revitalize our country in a dynamic way!"

The crowd roared in support of the statement.

"In fact, I have a better idea." Philip said excitedly, "Let's make the Philippines not just a venue for these refugees but a venue for the entire world. Let's welcome all immigrants, entrepreneurs, students and create not just one but several living communities throughout the country! Let's truly open our borders and lead the way towards true global citizenship!"

There was pandemonium in the room.

Philip realized there was no way this conversation can continue. This issue was way beyond a conversation. It would require a much larger discussion. He would need the support of the entire congress and senate—as well as the President. In fact, leaders from several countries and international organizations have to be involved. This was no longer just a political skirmish; this was a global war against the oppression of refugees.

The President of the Philippines decided to take in the refugees and keep them in camps while the political decision relating to their fate had not been resolved.

Philip and his team proposed for a bill not just to relocate refugees to the living communities but to also open the country's border and initiate an open-door policy for immigrants all over the world. Philip underscored the fact that America became a great country partly due to its diversity and talented immigrants.

He proposed a similar model for the Philippines, but a better one. Immigrants and refugees will not just be taken in; they will be groomed to have successful careers and endeavors and actively participate in economic revitalization. Each immigrant will take this pledge upon entering the country.

Philip's proposed bill and international campaign in recent months had been a roller-coaster ride. The past 2 weeks had been promising. The Philippine congress and senate passed his proposed bill. He also received overwhelming support from the international community. His living community model received over $100 billion in funding from countries and international organizations around the world. In fact, other countries worldwide have decided to study the model and explore its implementation.

Working late in his office one night, the phone rang. It was from the U.S. President.

He listened intently at what the U.S. President had to say.

He smiled and said, "Yes, Mr. President. I'd be happy to send you a copy of the feasibility plan of the proposed living community."

Legacy Lesson 3: Politics can be a real platform for change.

Art courtesy of Allison Brannon

CHAPTER 4

Evie Roberts:
Intellectual Legacy

It is up to us to live up to the legacy that was left for us, and to leave a legacy that is worthy of our children and of future generations.
—Christine Gregoire

Evie Roberts shuffled the papers in her hand. She was stressed and harassed. Much like her other classmates in the Master in Computer Science program at the University of Oxford in the UK.

She looked at her notes again to make sure nothing was amiss in the artificial intelligence algorithm she created. A perfectionist, she makes it a point to review her work multiple times before sharing it with others. She grasped the file tightly. This was the biggest project in her life, perhaps one that would redefine the field of artificial intelligence.

Professor John Smith, an elderly gentleman who's a renowned global authority in artificial intelligence, pored over the only duplicate copy of her file. He was seated in a large swivel chair by a mahogany desk right in front of her. As her project mentor, he aimed to assist her in ensuring everything was professionally done and accurate.

While waiting, Evie pored over the diplomas, awards, and certifications that adorned the professor's office. "What a highly accomplished man," she thought. "I'd be happy to accomplish a tenth of what he's accomplished. Heck, even if it were just a hundredth—it would still be an amazing career."

Evie was somewhat tense. If Professor Smith rejects her model, she would have to start from scratch. It could take her many more months, perhaps years, to create another viable algorithm. Again, with uncertain results. This would mean piling up more student debt and taking odd jobs to pay for the bills. She was not getting any younger. Many of her contemporaries already had stable jobs and senior management roles.

A loner who's been mathematically gifted, she loved numbers and logic. The field of computer science, especially artificial intelligence, has been a mental and physical abode. Discovering this field of study somewhat later in life brought her much elation. She finally found her passion.

Mathematical and computer programming gave her a sense of purpose. It was clear and it was measurable—unlike many things in life. She had failed miserably in other careers such as sales executive and customer service representative, but this one she knew she could excel. Her objective was not just to be the best in her class, but to be the best in the world. In fact, she wanted something even bigger. She wanted to revolutionize the field of artificial intelligence.

Professor John Smith was reading the document intently and started shaking his head.

"Oh no," Evie pondered fearfully, "I must have done something wrong. This could be a total disaster."

She was so nervous, she wanted to cry. She had put so much work on the project. His feedback would make or break her chances for her post-graduate degree completion. This was truly a career defining moment. She started to regret the decisions she made. Negative thoughts started to flood her mind, "I should have picked an easier project. Why did I have to be so ambitious? Why did I have to pick something so radical and disruptive?"

Professor Smith placed the file down slowly in the table and stared at Evie.

"Well" he said, "You certainly are aspiring for the extraordinary aren't you?"

Evie's heart raced. "What does that mean?" she thought. "Was this project out of bounds and undoable?"

She deliberated for a moment and replied, "I wanted to do something meaningful. A model that could protect many companies from the risks and hazards brought about by artificial intelligence. As mentioned in my rationale, cybersecurity is not enough."

Professor Smith nodded and said, "I think it's the work of a genius. My only concern is the pushback from many companies who have already invested heavily in artificial intelligence. Your model challenges the norm and all the perceived benefits associated with artificial intelligence."

Evie quickly jumped on. "I do not argue that artificial intelligence is not useful. I argue that in almost any institutional framework in the world—such as politics, law, economics—there has to be some check and balance. It should be the same for artificial intelligence. There needs to be a mechanism for correction and order."

"I can see that," Professor Smith responded, "What you are proposing in the creation of an Anti-AI, a nemesis for artificial intelligence. An algorithm with a set logic that would correct artificial programming once it exhibits dark tendencies or a propensity for disorder."

"Exactly," Evie added. "It would be like a dormant, unseen superhero that would step in once things go awfully wrong. For example, when a robot starts to breach security in a government facility to access nuclear weapons, the program will kick in and block it completely."

Professor Smith rubbed his chin pensively, "Who would oversee it then? Who would monitor it? The United Nations? Would a council manage it? Or a group of select nations and their spy agencies? In such case, the programs created give those with access an unfair advantage over the others wouldn't it?"

Evie smiled, "I completely agree. That's why they wouldn't be on the know."

Professor Smith was baffled. "Who would know then?"

Evie continued, "You remember the Bitcoin model right? Did anybody ever find out who the unknown creator dubbed as Satoshi Nakamoto was? Never! It rolled out secretly around the world and provided and revolutionized digital currency forever."

Professor Smith was very intrigued. "So, who would know?"

Evie winked at him, "Just you and me."

Professor Smith was amazed, "What?"

Evie continued, "Professor, you taught me the importance of ethics in artificial intelligence. You taught me of the need to be constantly innovative and to think outside the box. You taught me about the importance of cybersecurity.

This model converges everything you taught me. Knowing how strongly you feel about responsible automation, as well as your high inclination towards privacy and secrecy, I thought we can keep this little secret together."

Professor Smith laughed. "You never cease to surprise me. A technical question, if it's secret then you can't submit this as your class project."

Evie smiled again, "I already thought about that. I've created a tamed down version of the model excluding its real intent. Do you really think the model works? Will I get good marks for the project?

Professor Smith quickly responded, "You will get the highest marks for the project. And, yes I think the model works."

Evie stood up close to the professor and whispered, "I'm glad you think it works. I will unleash Anti-AI tomorrow.

Legacy Lesson 4: Use your intelligence to change the game.

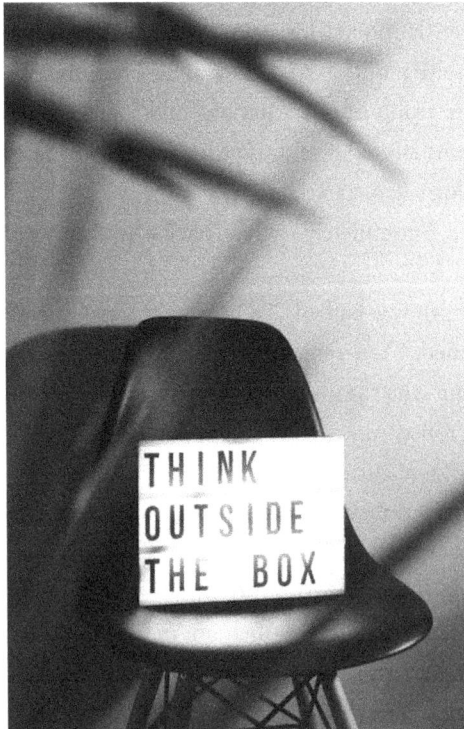

Art courtesy of Allison Brannon

CHAPTER 5

Antonio Barbosa: Spiritual Legacy

The greatest legacy one can pass on to one's children and grandchildren is not money or material things accumulated in one's life, but rather a legacy of character and faith.

—Billy Graham

One of the largest newspapers in Brazil, *Folha de Sao Paulo*, had this title in one of its headlines "Antonio Barbosa proposes multi-religiosity." The news article was covered in all sorts of media—print, radio, television, and the web. In fact, it wasn't just in the local media, it was talked about by various international media all over the world.

His approach to religion fascinated the entire global community. He founded a religious movement called "*Uma Igreja*" meaning one church. He believed in the consolidation rather than fragmentation of religion. He believed that by consolidating resources across religious groups more lives will be touched and uplifted.

In a recent interview, he said, "All over the world, we have shortages of priests. We have shortages of churches. Each religion is pushing its own agenda forward. In reality, we have only one creator, one God. Why don't we consolidate our effort and resources to make an impact on more lives? Isn't that what religion is all about? Salvation, love, peace? I'd love to see religions around the world work with each other not against each other."

His interview made waves all over the world. Some religious leaders hated his vision, others loved it. Many religions have seen a decline in church attendance and participation, why not embrace everyone, manage available infrastructure better, and profess a common message of love. As an example, some Catholic churches in far-flung communities barely survive because of lack of priests. Why not use the same facility to hosts Mormons or Muslims? Mormons and Muslims can return the favor in other locations. A church stands as a symbol of God, regardless of your faith. We are one global, spiritual community.

Media reactions on his interviews were varied. Some believed he was a contemporary prophet with a vision truly attuned with the times. Others thought he was out of his mind convinced that protectionist tendencies of religious groups would never give way to the notion of consolidation.

Jim Brown of the *New York Times* was excited at the chance of meeting Antonio Barbosa. He was at Antonio's home an hour before the interview time. When he got a chance to meet him, he couldn't help firing away questions the global audience really wanted to hear. He was truly thankful that he had a competent interpreter with him ready to assist with the translation.

Brown: Thank you, Mr. Barbosa, for having this interview with me.

Barbosa: You're most welcome, Mr. Brown. I'm delighted to help enlighten your readers on the vision of Uma Igreja.

Brown: Please tell me, how did you come about founding Uma Igreja?

Barbosa: Since my youth, I have always been spiritual. As a young executive, I traveled to many remote places on my company's behalf. On many occasions, I couldn't find a Catholic church. At one point, it dawned upon me. Why can't I just pray in a Mormon church? We have one God anyway, right? I'm sure, our creator will listen to me whether I'm in a Catholic church, a Muslim mosque, or a Jewish synagogue.

Over the years, I ended up visiting and praying in all religious places. In all places I visited, I felt very much welcome. In fact, I had a similar spiritual feeling everywhere I went. Eventually, I passed on the message to friends and family. Many loved the concept and started to turn to me as a leader in consolidating religion worldwide.

Brown: It seems like you now have quite a following. How many members do you have thus far?

Barbosa: I never count membership. My spiritual philosophy is open to everyone. Followers can come and leave as they please. If our YouTube channel is any indication, we have around fifty million followers worldwide. Again, participation is non-binding. You can still practice whatever religion you want. My approach is more anchored on a pragmatic movement to combine resources across religion and enrich more lives.

Brown: Have you established a formal partnership with other religions at this point?

Barbosa: No, it was never about structuring formal relationships, it was always about mutual cooperation to achieve common goals across religions. In business, you may have heard the term "strategic alliances." This is a situation where companies retain their complete autonomy yet work together to accomplish common goals. This is my vision on how religions worldwide can work together.

Brown: What are your plans for the future?

Barbosa: I want to continue this movement and impact as many lives as I can. I really think religions can and should work together—and think in new and creative ways—to best serve their followers. With many religions facing mounting challenges and constraints, a new level of global cooperation is necessary.

Brown: Do you have a message you'd like to impart to our global readers?

Barbosa: Make an effort to uplift your spirit. It doesn't matter what religion you belong to. We are all the same in the eyes of our creator. Please be respectful of other religions too. It truly breaks my heart whenever I hear of a bombing or shooting in a place of worship. The victims were there worshiping the same God we all pray to. Over the centuries, religions have evolved. In the past century, our society has too changed in dramatic ways. Shouldn't religion evolve as well?

Legacy Lesson 5: Spiritual conviction can make a difference.

Art courtesy of Allison Brannon

CHAPTER 6

Neha Anand: Cultural Legacy

Legacy is not leaving something for people. It's leaving something in people.

—Peter Strople

It was just after the crack of dawn in Calcutta, India and Neha Anand has just stepped out of her tiny apartment to get to work. Her call center supervisor has assigned her the early morning shift this week. She didn't mind. She enjoyed doing customer service work and in helping others understand and appreciate technology. In her job, she gets to answer and respond to customer requests from all over the world, mostly from America.

Yesterday was such a busy day, she resolved almost ten customer problems each hour. She prides herself for being consistently polite, dependable, and efficient.

The only setback in her work was her pay. Despite working so hard and doing frequent overtime work, she could hardly make ends meet. For a few years now, she had been living close to a hand-to-mouth existence. Much like several nations across the world, the cost of living had gone up while salaries have remained at the same level.

She took a deep breath to calm her mind. She proceeded to walk briskly toward the already bustling streets of Calcutta.

She glanced at the vendors already setting up their stalls to sell products for the day. For some, it was bread. For others, it was specialty food like *phuchka*. And for others, services such as haircuts. She always had a high regard for entrepreneurs. Their work ethic, courage to face risk and uncertainty, bootstrapping and creative flair to generate any form of profit intrigued her.

As a young girl, she dreamt of being an entrepreneur. She wanted to have her own small business, create jobs in Calcutta, and perhaps help transform the lives of many. "How did this dream end?" she wondered, "Could I possibly still start a business at some point in my life?"

She continued walking toward her office. From the corner of her eye, she spotted a teenage girl painting a beautiful graffiti art on the wall. "What a wonderful image," she thought "What a captivating cultural representation of India!"

She decided to talk to the girl. She was very impressed by her art, but more so her courage. While laws on vandalism were hardly enforced, she still could get into trouble. She was touched by the fact that the beautiful artwork added beauty to the street. Seeing such art would brighten the day of many pedestrians.

She stood close to the girl and said, "You make such beautiful art! What's your name?"

The girl was somewhat startled, but relaxed when she saw Neha. "Thank you... I'm Shanaya."

Neha was curious, "What made you decide to do such painting on the wall?"

Shanaya replied softly, "I don't have a canvas and I found some extra paint from my neighbor's shop."

The A-ha Moment

Her response hit Neha like a ton of bricks. She was speechless. She felt a rage build inside of her. "How can we waste so much talent around the world because of poverty?" She thought "How can countries miss on a golden opportunity to showcase their art and culture? Something needs to get done. I need to help."

Neha took a photo of the graffiti and got Shanaya's home address. They agreed to meet and discuss an art project.

While at work, Neha couldn't get Shanaya of her mind. "How many Shanayas are out there in the world? So many talented artists didn't have a proper venue for their craft."

Back home that night, she decided to do something about it. She realized that in life we could either watch things happen or make things happen. She had merely watched things all of her life. She went through the motions and all the hustle and bustle. Now she wanted to lead something. This was the time and moment to do something significant and pursue her entrepreneurial dream.

Neha started typing up a business plan for a web platform called Efitti or e-graffiti. The idea was to create a giant virtual wall in a website where artists can either upload a picture of their art or simply express themselves by freely painting their own graffiti. Any artist or art enthusiast from around the world can participate. In fact, everyone can participate. One can scribble in an "I love you" text and refer the wall coordinates (line and row number) to a loved one. Why not democratize art and allow everyone an opportunity to express themselves virtually!

The Disruption

Efitti will be like Facebook, but with a personal, artistic touch. It will be a subscription service. It will be free for most users, but professionals who need more space to display their craft would pay a rent for wall usage. There would also be space for advertisements. In order for this socially driven enterprise to be sustainable, there had to be an income stream.

The business plan was a mere start. In the coming months, Neha rallied a few friends to help her kickoff E-fitti. She set up a formal company to pursue this dream. Shanaya became her poster child, with much of her amazing art prominently displayed as an example for others.

The number of users has reached millions in just a few months.

Neha prides herself the most not just for the venture's success, but her ability to showcase Indian art and culture to the world. She is very pleased by the participation of art enthusiasts from many other countries. In her own small way, she managed to start a cultural revolution.

Legacy Lesson 6: Cultural transformation is a tool for rapid change with the convergence of technology and globalization.

Art courtesy of Allison Brannon

CHAPTER 7

Emilio Rodriguez: Physical Legacy

I don't fight for the money. I fight for my legacy. I fight for history. I fight for my people.

——Khabib Nurmagomedov, UFC Champion

The stocky 18-year-old youth shook the punching bag with his hard and extremely fast punches. His trainer can hardly hold on. He wasn't known as "*El Relampago*" or "The lighting" in Mexico for nothing.

Despite his 5 ft 10 in height and body weight of 210 lb, the speed with which he moved across the ring is simply amazing.

Magic Ingredient

Emilio Rodriguez has been described in boxing magazines as "Mike Tyson ++." His boxing style and power is a replica of boxing legend Mike Tyson in his youth. There is an added "magic ingredient" in his abilities—lightning speed. He has an uncanny ability to disappear from the line of sight of his opponents and suddenly bombard them with five to ten power punches. Few ever survived his attacks.

Despite his very young age, he already has a professional boxing record of 25–0. All 25 wins have been by way of knockout in under five rounds.

Emilio has been in the global stage in recent months as a result of his lined up first title fight for the World Boxing Association (WBA) heavyweight championship of the world. If he wins, he would make history by being the youngest heavy champion of the world.

There has been a lot of speculation about his ability. Many experts claimed that aside from his last five fights, his past opponents were not world-class fighters. He built his record from mere luck and for fighting weak opponents. Yet many remained impressed, his skill and professionalism at such a young age has not been typical in the world of boxing.

When Talent Meets Destiny

Emilio's trainer Ernesto called him to one side and handed him a glass of water. "So, how do you feel? Do you feel up to it?"

Emilio took a sip of water and threw some speed punches in the air, "You know I'm born for this Ernesto. When it's your destiny, and you're blessed from above, everything is easy."

Ernesto smiled. He had always been impressed by Emilio's strong faith. The boxer would pay for five masses before each fight. He would pray that his fight would end in less than five rounds. So far, his prayers have been consistently answered. Ernesto was concerned about the upcoming fight though. The current heavy champion was a lot bigger than Emilio. He was undefeated with a record of 45 wins, with 40 by way of knockout.

Emilio and the current champion had different boxing styles. Emilio tends to be the aggressor, the champion tends to be a slugger. Emilio's strength is speed, the champion's strength is power. On several occasions, the champion's left hook threw the opponent a couple of feet up the air. Seven of the champion's opponents have been hospitalized after the fight.

Emilio's camp was worried about this fight. This was the biggest fight in Emilio's young life. There was a huge risk, yet the rewards were very high. Emilio had the opportunity to become the youngest heavyweight champion of the world.

The path to his boxing success was not an easy one. Emilio had a rough life as a young child. He grew up in poverty and often got into trouble with neighborhood thugs. Some say, he acquired his speed by warding off simultaneous attacks of multiple thugs. Emilio's neighborhood still recount the days when as an 8-year-old boy, he single-handedly fought six grown men and knocked them all out.

He had to drop out of school multiple times to try to make some money. The fact that his father was in prison meant that he had to somehow help his mom bring food to the table. He did odd jobs like working in the grocery store to make some money. He soon discovered that he can earn more by taking part in weekly underground, bare-knuckle fights. He learned to fight the hard way. At that point in life, he had no boxing training whatsoever. He threw and took punches like a man. He learned and mastered the art of street-fighting.

His life took a positive turn when Ernesto spotted him in one of the underground fighting events. He took the young man under his wing, trained him, and introduced him to the top boxing manager in Mexico. The rest, as they say, is history.

Ernesto had a glimpse of Emilio's discipline and passion for the sport years back. Emilio asked him then, "How many hours a day do professional boxers work out?" Ernesto said it was 3 to 5 hours a day. Emilio shrugged and said, "I'd like to double that." He had never seen a committed boxer as Emilio in his entire life.

On one day, Ernesto asked, "Why do you train so hard?" Emilio looked at him intently and said, "I am destined to be a champion one day my friend. I'd like to be the best boxer in the world."

Emilio not only trained hard, he also studied hard. He wanted to learn everything he can. He read books about boxing and fitness. He spent countless hours watching boxing fights and training videos. He consulted with trainers, medical experts, and coaches from around the world. He wanted to be not only in his best physical shape but also his best mental and spiritual self. Aside from a doctor, a dietician, and a trainer, he even had a priest in his entourage.

In retrospect, it dawned upon Ernesto that all roads have led to this event. Emilio had been preparing for this upcoming fight all his life. Moreover, he had positive thoughts and prayers from all over Mexico backing him up. An entire nation was rooting for him.

A Night to Remember

The championship night finally came. The first ten rounds were fairly even between Emilio and the champion. The score cards showed that

Emilio performed better than the champion in the first five rounds. The champion was ahead on points from the sixth to the tenth round. The eleventh round was called a draw—both boxers knocked each other down.

The twelfth and final round was coming up. Emilio sat by his corner for a minute of rest. A doctor stopped by to examine his badly swollen and bleeding eye. Emilio assured the doctor he was okay. The reality was that he could not see at all from the swollen eye. Emilio was glad the doctor could not see his broken rib and sprained left hand. There is no quitting now. His destiny and legacy was on the line.

Ernesto was concerned, "Are you okay? Do you want to do this?"

Emilio nodded and smiled weakly, "You know I'll do this even if I have to die in this ring tonight right?"

Ernesto looked at Emilio closely, "Look, you'll need a knockout to win. The fight is too close to call. Some score cards may show the champ leading slightly on points. You really need to knock him out."

Emilio nodded slowly and did not respond. He worked so hard for this fight. He had given it his heart and soul. His extensive training helped him endure the brutal punches of the champion. If he had trained just a tad less, he would have been knocked out several rounds earlier. He contemplated on how he can knock out the champion. His body was aching, but he tried to keep his mind of the pain. He wondered whether the champion was also in pain like him. He looked at the champion to see if there was any indication of pain or weakness. He noticed that the champion was rubbing his hand over his right abdomen and speaking to his trainer about it and he was grimacing in pain. Emilio smiled, he found the champion's weaknesses—a broken rib on the right side. He'll throw the hardest punch he could ever throw in that spot.

The bell rang signaling the start of round 12.

As the two boxers approached each other, Emilio immediately ducked, shifted to the right and with a lightning speed threw a solid right blow to the right abdomen of the champion. The champion did not know what hit him. The champion instantly fell on his knees and could no longer stand up.

The crowd roared and erupted in amazement and cheers.

The fight was stopped and Emilio was declared the winner.

Emilio was immediately propelled to the global stage. He solidified his legacy. Hours after the heavyweight championship fight, newspapers worldwide read, "Rodriguez becomes youngest heavyweight champ."

Legacy Lesson 7: There exist opportunities to leverage one's physical attributes, strength, stamina, skills, and raw talent to make an impact.

Art courtesy of Allison Brannon

CHAPTER 8

James Turner: Historical Legacy

The leader of an Earth organization who makes a commitment to history—of humans living on Earth, to begin permanent settlement/ occupation of not the moon, but of another planet—this leader will have a legacy for history that will supersede Columbus, Genghis Khan or almost any recognized leader.

—Buzz Aldrin

James Turner pored over the map and pointed to the exact spot he wanted to be to the boat's captain Bill George.

The duo had worked together in past expeditions. But this was their most ambitious quest ever.

They were in a spot in the Pacific Ocean known as the Challenger Deep in the Mariana Trench. It had a confirmed depth of about 10,994 m or approximately 36,070 ft. It is the deepest point of the earth's ocean. In fact, if Mt. Everest's height of 29,029 ft were placed on this location, it would remain covered by over a mile of water.

In the past 5 years, James had made it his mission to explore the depth of Challenger Deep. In his funding proposal, he argued that instead of spending billions of dollars in space expedition, we should be spending the money to explore our oceans. There were abundant sea life to still discover and much had to be understood about the impact the ocean had on events that directly impact our lives like earthquakes and rise in sea level.

As a young child, James was fascinated by famed explorers like Christopher Columbus, Marco Polo, and Ferdinand Magellan. He admired their courage in taking expeditions in uncharted waters. He was impressed by their ability to rally for support and to lead men in such a challenging and dangerous endeavor. Most of all, he was thrilled by the fact that they made history and will forever be remembered for their feat.

His more recent idols were Jacques Piccard and Don Walsh, the hydronauts who first explored and descended into the Challenger Deep on January 23, 1960. They boarded the Bathyscaphe Trieste submersible sea vessel and reached approximately 10,916 m into the earth's ocean.

Piccard and Walsh made history by being the only two people who have traveled to the bottom of the Mariana Trench. Since the Plexiglas window had cracked during their descent, the men only spent roughly 20 minutes in the sea floor. Despite their very short visit, they were able to convey to the world exactly what they saw. The sea floor was filled with dark brown matter and abundant sea life consisting of shrimp and fish.

In more recent decades, unmanned crafts were used to explore the Challenger Deep—the Kaiko exploration in the 1990s and the Nereus in 2009.

James Turner's goal was to be the third man ever to descend into the Challenger Deep. But what he had in mind was far loftier. Rather than spending a mere few minutes in the deepest part of the ocean, he intended to spend 1 month in the deepest part of the earth's ocean to observe, conduct research, and report his findings. With new technology available, he would also be able to do a live broadcast of what he sees to the world.

James truly felt this mission was a culminating event of his entire life's work. He had served in the U.S. Navy, had bachelor and postgraduate degrees in oceanography, and has emerged as a global expert in his field with numerous published journal articles and books. He had been a keynote speaker in major oceanography conferences and his past ocean exploits have been consistently successful.

The only disappointment James had at this point is that his mission was not funded by the U.S. government. He would have preferred to take on this feat as an added source and pride for his home country. After several months of searching, he found a private investor. He felt extremely fortunate to have acquired all the resources he needed from the billionaire philanthropist Michael Smith.

He decided to call Michael Smith before he made the historic decent.

Michael immediately picked up the phone, "Hey, everything going well James?"

James pulled the phone closer to hear Michael better, "Yes, all is good. I just wanted to call you. We're making history, my friend."

Michael was quiet for several seconds, he was somewhat concerned. "All safety and security protocol in place? All technology double-checked?"

James nodded, "Yes, sir. All's good and ready to go."

Michael was excited, "This is going to be big. The world is never going to forget this."

James never passed up an opportunity to show his gratitude to Michael, "Thank you so much for your support, Michael."

Michael quickly replied, "No, I should say thank you to you, James. I couldn't think of a more qualified person to lead this expedition. It's been a pleasure working with you. I'm honored to be a part of it. I guess in some way, I'm glad the U.S. government didn't want to be involved. Otherwise, we would not have come across each other."

Both men laughed.

While the expedition was very well planned, both men knew there were risks involved.

After a brief moment of silence, Michael spoke, "Good luck, James, and God bless."

James smiled, "Thank you, Michael. I'll make sure you'll have the first human selfie at the bottom of the earth." Both laughed and said their goodbyes.

Immediately after, James called his wife and children and conveyed his love. They were excited about his involvement in such a momentous event. They wished him well knowing that this was his ultimate dream and life's passion. They said a simple prayer together.

James ended the call and looked at the vast expanse of the ocean. It will be a month before he'll see the ocean's surface again. He proceeded to enter the sea vessel.

"Well, are you ready?" Captain Bill George asked.

"More than ever," James said smiling, as he sealed the vessel's door.

His descent into the Challenger Deep was broadcasted live worldwide. For the first time ever, the world was able to see exactly what James saw in the deepest part of the ocean. He made history in many levels: (1) for being the third man to descend into the Challenger Deep, (2) for having stayed in the deepest ocean floor the longest, and (3) for arranging the first ever human live broadcast from the bottom of the ocean.

And, yes—Michael got the historic selfie.

Legacy Lesson 8: Create your own history.

Art courtesy of Allison Brannon

CHAPTER 9

Lessons from the Stories

Lives of great people remind us we can make our lives sublime and, departing, leave behind footprints in the sand of time.

—Henry Longfellow

Eight stories were featured in this book. These inspirational stories offer a learning point that can help us think about potential ways where we too can create a legacy and make a lasting impact. Each story serves as a legacy guide that we can follow.

Table 9.1 reviews each of the story protagonist, the type of legacy, and the lesson learned.

Table 9.1 Summary of legacy lessons

Lesson	Person	Legacy type	Lesson learned
Lesson 1	Jack Wilson	Financial legacy	Leverage your financial resources to make an impact.
Lesson 2	Aya Rahal	Social legacy	Use social capital to make a dramatic change.
Lesson 3	Philip Gomez	Political legacy	Politics can be a real platform for change.
Lesson 4	Evie Roberts	Intellectual legacy	Use your intelligence to change the game.
Lesson 5	Antonio Barbosa	Spiritual legacy	Spiritual conviction can make a difference.
Lesson 6	Neha Anand	Cultural legacy	Cultural transformation is a tool for rapid change with the convergence of technology and globalization.
Lesson 7	Emilio Rodriguez	Physical legacy	There exist opportunities to leverage one's physical attributes, strength, stamina, skills, and raw talent to make an impact.
Lesson 8	James Turner	Historical legacy	Create your own history.

As shown in Table 9.1, as human beings, we are in a position to pursue diverse forms of legacy and make a lasting impact in our own way.

The featured lessons have implications for all of us—whether you're a student, a businessman, an employee, or even a retiree. It applies to everyone from all walks of life. Table 9.2 highlights the executive implications of the legacy lessons.

The insights from Table 9.2 suggest that we are living at a time and in a society that enables all of us to accomplish unparalleled feats. We are in a position to make a real difference in our world. We face the option

Table 9.2 Executive implications of the legacy lessons

Legacy lesson	Executive implications
Leverage your financial resources to make an impact.	Executives have financial resources, large or small, at their disposal. Make those resources work to impact society in some way.
Use social capital to make a dramatic change.	Networks, relationships, and friendships can advance a legacy goal at a hyper speed. When done right, social media and web platforms can be very helpful in this process.
Politics can be a real platform for change.	While involvement in politics can have its ups and downs, collaborating and communicating effectively with political leaders could provide a stimulus for real change to take place.
Use your intelligence to change the game.	The potential of the human mind is endless. Utilizing the mind to pursue groundbreaking ideas can lead to phenomenal results.
Spiritual conviction can make a difference.	Religion nurtures the human spirit. Pursuing one's spiritual development while making an impact on the lives of others can be truly fulfilling.
Cultural transformation is a tool for rapid change with the convergence of technology and globalization.	Advancements in technology have made the world a much smaller place. Implementing cultural changes in a personal, corporate, and societal level can take place very quickly.
There exist opportunities to leverage one's physical attributes, strength, stamina, skills, and raw talent to make an impact.	Breakthroughs in medicine and health care have set the stage for the optimization of the human body and its performance. Capitalizing on these developments can take one's physicality to an entirely new level.
Create your own history.	World history is filled with amazing personalities and stories of groundbreaking achievements. The actions we take today sets the foundation for tomorrow's history—make it count.

of either watching things happen or making things happen. If you are looking to create a lasting legacy, this era and this generation is the perfect time to make things happen.

While there are several executive implications from the featured stories that set the foundation for action, there are additional insights from the stories that can help enrich one's legacy. Here are some noteworthy considerations:

1. **Different legacy for each person.** The stories in this book point out to the fact that individuals have different talents, abilities, and resources that they can use to find meaning in their lives and to make an impact. A viable approach would be to use what you have and leverage it in the best way you can. The featured story characters had different strengths and faced different circumstances. Moreover, they were located in different parts of the world. Yet, they accomplished a common feat—they created an amazing legacy. They were able to create initiatives of Very High Memorial Capacity (VHMC). You may wonder What if I don't have much talent or resources, would I still be able to enrich my legacy? Some of the characters in the book such as Neha Anand had modest talent and very limited resources. Yet, in Neha's case building on a creative idea and passion, she was able to develop a meaningful enterprise that led to a powerful cultural legacy.

2. **Legacy needs to be aligned with purpose and mission.** Several characters in the book had experiences in their lives that led to their finding of a relevant purpose and mission. For example, as a young boy, James Turner was fascinated by explorers. Billionaire Jack Wilson nearly drowned and was saved by sea gypsies. Their early experiences helped shape their future mission and legacy.

   For many of us, many seemingly random and inconsequential events may appear initially meaningless. In the end, these events can evolve into something bigger and can define a future mission or goal. As human beings, it is in our DNA to be helpful to others. This propensity to do good and assist fellow human beings has been observed in several scientific and social experiments.

3. **Plan for your legacy.** The characters in this book concretized their legacy not by chance but through careful planning. For example, Philip Gomez, the Philippine senator who pushed for open migration, spent months planning for and lobbying to the local and international communities. Careful planning improves your chances of creating a powerful legacy. The creation of a Strategic Legacy Plan (SLP) considering the mission and goals, implementing team, market environment, resources required, timeline and process of implementation would be very helpful.

4. **Impact matters.** A common theme in the stories of this book is the scale, scope, and magnitude of impact of the characters. They have all pursued and executed a course of action that led to a powerful legacy and had a VHMC or better. For example, Evie Robert's creation of the Anti-AI would have a profound impact on the world. You may be thinking, I'm just an ordinary Jack or Jill working in a 9 to 5 job, how can I ever make a meaningful impact?

   You actually can. Small acts of goodness could actually lead to something significant in another person's life. As a clerk, the job interview you efficiently facilitated may have led to an applicant's job that eventually transformed his life and that of his family's. As a nurse, that extra effort you placed on double checking the patient's vitals may have saved a life and facilitated another person's legacy. As a teacher, that small lesson you imparted one day could help a student excel in her work or contribute to society.

   Not all of us are destined to make an amazing impact. But, our dedication to our work, our friends and family, provides a framework for a level of impact that truly matters.

5. **Timing is key.** When one implements his or her legacy matters. For example, Aya Rahal, the accidental gay rights activist, may not have been successful if she set up her web and app platform 20 years ago. Often times, the condition has to be right for a meaningful legacy to be implemented, In Evie's case, the convergence of available technology, an evolving social mindset, and cultural transformation paved the way for her success. For some of us, our legacy may just be around the corner, for others it may take more time. Billionaire Jack Wilson, the Australian businessmen, found his legacy much later in

life. It does not matter whether we find our legacy early or late. What is essential is that we find it at some point in our lives in order to find our true purpose and happiness.

6. **Creativity makes a difference.** The stories in this book underscore the importance of creativity and innovativeness in the quest for one's legacy. Antonio Barbosa, the game-changer of religion, took on an entirely new approach on religion. In many cases, rethinking what is conventional can lead to an exciting legacy pathway. In our small way, introducing an innovation or out-of-the box thinking can lead to an important social impact.

   As a sales manager, finding ways to extend more credit for clients can help augment their income and improve family finances. As a school administrator, identifying a discount scheme to minimize student loans can help many complete their education. As ordinary human beings, we are all poised to make some level of difference in our own way. The bigger question is whether we make an actual effort to think about it and make things happen.

7. **Engage others.** Several stories in the book showcase the need to engage others when enriching your legacy. Emilio Rodriguez, the boxer, had Ernesto his trainer who helped him. Explorer James Turner had Captain Bill George who provided key assistance. Gay activist Aya Rahal had her cousin Ahmed who provided the technological and entrepreneurial spin to her endeavor. Explorer James Turner had billionaire investor Michael Smith who funded his expedition.

   It is difficult for us to enrich our legacies by ourselves. We need others to help us. It is important to understand that a legacy is rarely a solo flight. It requires a team effort, a strong commitment from others in order to succeed.

8. **Implementation is important.** It is fairly easy to come up with great ideas. What really makes a difference is how it is executed. The characters in this book had exciting ideas that concretized their legacy. But more than just ideas, they had the ability and solid plan to execute it. Evie Roberts spent months researching and planning to make sure her plans were properly implemented. Emilio the boxer spent months preparing for his championship fight. When thinking about our legacy, consider its proper implementation.

Every day, thousands of ideas worldwide are generated, only few come into fruition. Those that get transformed from a mere dream to reality are backed by a solid plan of implementation.

9. **Challenges exist.** The pursuit of a legacy is not one without challenges. Oftentimes, tough obstacles have to be overcome before achieving success. Emilio had to face a formidable opponent in the ring. Congressman Philip Gomez had a tough opponent named Augusto Bonifacio. It is important to plan for tough challenges and strive to overcome them.

10. **Stay the course.** The stories suggest that the path to legacy enrichment is not always a straight line. Obstacles exists and the goal post changes. Those that have a VHMC or better demonstrate resiliency and adaptability. At times, they revise or update their plans to achieve their goals. James Turner faced a major setback by a failed attempt to get support from the U.S. government. By persevering, and in finding Michael Smith, a private investor, he was able to achieve his goal. We all have an exciting opportunity to enrich our legacy and make a global impact. The conditions may not be perfect at the moment, but if we persevere, the right time will eventually come.

As we go through life, we meet certain people and live through certain experiences. The people and experiences at times have brought much joy, at other times a lot of pain. What we have lived through sets the foundation for our life's meaning and ultimate legacy. As they say, there's a reason for everything. The lessons from the stories suggest that there is a way to overcome tough obstacles when you are pursuing your true destiny. All of us have our own mission in life. Some of us have found it, others are still searching. Some of us have big missions, others small. Regardless of the case, finding your passion and legacy are the keys that would unlock your true happiness and sense of fulfillment in life.

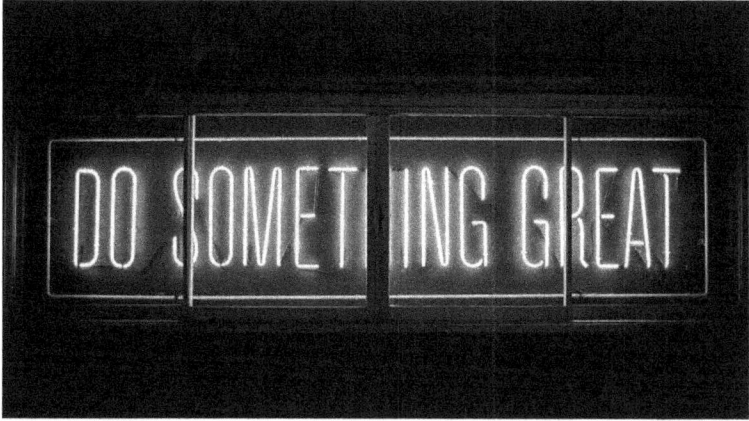

Art courtesy of Allison Brannon

CHAPTER 10

Planning for Your Legacy

The greatest gift is a portion of thyself.
—Ralph Waldo Emerson

The lessons from the stories underscore the importance of legacy planning. This chapter delves into what needs to be considered when planning for your legacy and in making a significant impact.

It all starts by understanding oneself and in asking the right questions. Table 10.1 offers a few suggestions on the type of questions you can ask yourself when contemplating your legacy.

Finding answers to the questions in Table 10.1 would help through the process of finding a suitable legacy for you. You may pick one or two or even several of the legacy options. The best legacy track for you will largely depend on your available resources, abilities, and motivation to make an impact.

Table 10.1 Questions for assessing your legacy

Financial	• How much resources do I have? • How can I best leverage these resources to make a meaningful impact? • What other resources can I attract? • Who would benefit the most from these resources? • What should I prioritize? • What would be the impact of these resources?
Social	• What is the current state of my social capital? • How can it be further enhanced? • What partnerships and alliances can help strengthen my social capital? • What are the best mediums to use? • How can my social capital be optimized? • What should I prioritize? • What impact would my social capital create?

(continued)

Table 10.1 Continued

Political	• What is my current political strength? • What areas can I improve on? • How can I best leverage my relationships to make an impact? • What issues should I focus on? • What should be my priorities? • What would be the impact of my courses of action?
Intellectual	• What is my intellectual strength? • How can I leverage this strength to make a meaningful impact? • What training, development, or resources do I need to optimize my intellectual capacity? • Who should I partner with? • What should I focus on? • What would be the impact of my courses of action?
Spiritual	• What are my spiritual beliefs? • What are my goals? • What changes do I want to make? • What agenda do I want to advance? • What resources do I need to make it happen? • What would be the impact of my courses of action?
Cultural	• What are my cultural anchors? • What do I want to change? • What resources do I need to make these changes happen? • What partnerships and alliances do I need? • What should be my priorities? • What would be the impact of my courses of action?
Physical	• What is my physical strength? • How can I leverage this strength along with my skills and abilities to make a meaningful impact? • What training, development, or resources do I need to optimize my physical prowess? • Who should I partner with? • What should I focus on? • What would be the impact of my courses of action?
Historical	• What are my historical anchors? • What historical impact do I want to make? • What resources do I need to make these changes happen? • What partnerships and alliances do I need? • What should be my priorities? • What would be the impact of my courses of action?

Once you've selected your legacy options, it would now be the time to plan for its implementation. I would recommend the use of a Strategic Legacy Plan (SLP). An SLP highlights tasks you need to consider when implementing your legacy. Table 10.2 discusses the components of the SLP.

Table 10.2 Strategic legacy plan (SLP)

Component	Description
Impact Model	The impact model refers to the depth, scale, scope, time, and inertia relating to the planned legacy initiative.
Goal Compatibility	Goal compatibility refers to the extent to which your identified goal is aligned with your planned legacy.
Market Environment	The market environment refers to the audience in which you intend to focus your legacy efforts.
Product/Service Suitability	Product/service suitability refers to how well matched your legacy product/service is with the audience you are looking to make an impact.
Management	Management refers to the personnel and key organizational players you intend to utilize to execute your legacy plan.
Marketing	Marketing refers to the promotion, sales, distribution, and public relations efforts you have in place to inform and engage your intended audience on your planned legacy.
Operations	Operations refers to the systems and processes you have in place to implement your legacy plan on a day-to-day basis.
Organizational Relationships	Organizational relationships refer to partnerships and alliances you intend to have with multiple stakeholders to implement your legacy plan.
Regulatory and Legal	Regulatory and legal aspects refer to the extent to which your legacy plan conforms with rule of law, ethics, as well government compliance issues.
Financial	Financial matters refer to monetary resources required to initiate and sustain your legacy plan.
Risk Assessment	Risk assessment refers to evaluation of hazards, risks, and challenges relating to the implementation of your legacy plan.
Review and Improvement	Review and improvement refers to the regular progress review and benchmarking of your legacy accomplishments as it relates to your established goals.

When creating an SLP, carefully weighing in on the components mentioned in Table 10.2 helps prevent the overlooking of obstacles relating to your plan.

In order to help you think through the components of the SLP, guide questions are offered in Table 10.3.

Table 10.3 Guide questions for the strategic legacy plan (SLP)

Component	Guide Questions
Impact Model	• What impact does your legacy model have with regard to depth, scale, scope, time, and inertia? • Has the model been tried elsewhere? • Why or why not? • How many lives will be impacted by your model? • How will it be best implemented? • When should it be implemented?
Goal Compatibility	• Is your legacy model aligned with your personal goals and objectives? • If not, what changes need to be made? • How would these changes be best implemented?
Market Environment	• Is your planned approach directed to the audience you wish to impact? • If not, what refinements are necessary? • How will these refinements be best implemented?
Product/Service Suitability	• Are you offering the right product or service to your target audience? • If not, what changes need to be made? • How would these changes be best implemented?
Management	• Do you have the right people who can help you execute your legacy plan well? • If not, what changes need to be made? • Do you have the resources ready? • Is the timing right?
Marketing	• Do you have the right marketing plan that will impact your audience and engage your stakeholders? • If not, what changes need to be made? • Do you have the resources ready? • Is the timing right?
Operations	• Do you have a viable system and process in place to execute your legacy plan well? • If not, what changes need to be made? • Do you have the resources ready? • Is the timing right?
Organizational Relationships	• What partnerships and alliances need to be in place to allow you to implement your legacy plan well? • If not, what changes need to be made? • How would these changes be best implemented?

Table 10.3 Continued

Component	Guide Questions
Regulatory and Legal	• What needs to be considered in terms of rule of law, ethics, as well government compliance issues? • What changes need to be made? • How would these changes be best implemented?
Financial	• What financial resources do you need to successfully implement your legacy plan? • What additional resources might you need? • How will these financial resources be best managed? • Who should manage them? • What checks and balances are in place?
Risk Assessment	• What hazards, risks, and challenges do you face in implementing the legacy plan? • How should these challenges be best addressed? • What resources are necessary?
Review and Improvement	• How will you review and improve your legacy plan? • How often should this be done? • Who should lead the process? • What benchmarks and standards should you follow?

Strategy is largely about actions executives take to accomplish their set goals. This applies to business activities and is equally relevant in legacy planning. The questions listed in Table 10.3 should be helpful in thinking through the implementation of your legacy plan.

Given the importance of the successful implementation of your legacy plan, Table 10.4 provides examples of action agenda you can pursue to transform your legacy plan from a mere dream into a reality.

Table 10.4 Action agenda for the strategic legacy plan (SLP)

Component	Action agenda
Impact Model	1. Do self-introspection and research to identify the area where you would like to create an impact. 2. Create a legacy model that clearly outlines the depth, scale, scope, time, and inertia relating to your plan. 3. Review the model with key partners, stakeholders, and implementers. 4. Test the model in a small scale. 5. Determine the timeline for your plan. 6. Secure resources to implement your plan on a large scale. 7. Implement your plan.

(*continued*)

Table 10.4 **Continued**

Component	Action agenda
Goal Compatibility	8. Determine if your legacy plan is aligned with your goals. 9. Make modifications as needed. 10. Review the plan and goals periodically to prevent mission drift.
Market Environment	11. Conduct research to ensure that your target sector is where you really want to make an impact on. 12. Speak with your target recipients and understand their needs. 13. Validate your findings with a third party. 14. Hire experts and consultants if necessary.
Product/Service Suitability	15. Conduct research to ensure the suitability of your product or service to the sector you want to make an impact on. 16. Speak with your target recipients and understand their needs. 17. Validate your findings with a third party. 18. Hire experts and consultants if necessary.
Management	19. Create an organizational chart to visually capture the manpower complement necessary to implement your plan. 20. Determine the timing of implementation. 21. Assess the resources and type of talent necessary to implement your plan well. 22. Recruit key people necessary for the efficient implementation of your plan. 23. Implement the plan. 24. Assess and review efficiency of your management process and team. 25. Plan for future manpower needs.
Marketing	26. Conduct research to determine marketing requirements. 27. Create a marketing plan relating to your legacy goals. 28. Review the plan with key partners, stakeholders, and implementers. 29. Assess resources necessary to implement the marketing plan. 30. Plan for the timing of implementation. 31. Implement the plan. 32. Assess and review the efficiency of your marketing process and team.
Operations	33. Create a flow chart to visually capture the process of your operations. 34. Ensure you have the right people and process in place. 35. Assess resources necessary for efficient operations. 36. Review and assess operations periodically. 37. Seek help of consultants and experts as needed. 38. Plan ahead for future operational needs.

Table 10.4 Continued

Component	Action agenda
Organizational Relationships	39. Identify partners and alliances necessary for the successful implementation of your legacy plan. 40. Create a structure for these relationships. 41. Approach partners and allies and concretize relationship agreements with them. 42. Plan for relationship arrangements both for the short term and long term. 43. Review the success of the relationship arrangements and make necessary changes down the road.
Regulatory and Legal	44. Conduct research and fully understand the legalities, ethics, and regulatory issues relating to your legacy plan. 45. Hire or consult with legal advisors and experts. 46. Ensure you have appropriate legal, ethical, and compliance matters in order. 47. Stay abreast with changes in the regulatory and legal environment. 48. Plan to go beyond just conforming with legal and ethical boundaries, strive to be a role model.
Financial	49. Conduct research to determine optimal financial practices. 50. Create a financial plan relating to your legacy goals. 51. Review the plan with key partners, stakeholders, and implementers. 52. Assess resources necessary to implement the financial plan. 53. Plan for the timing of implementation. 54. Implement the plan. 55. Assess and review the efficiency of your financial process and structure.
Risk Assessment	56. Conduct research and fully understand all hazards, risks, and challenges associated with your legacy plan. 57. Hire or consult with risk experts. 58. Ensure you have operational safeguards in place to minimize risk. 59. Stay abreast with the best practices in the industry. 60. Leverage technology and management systems to ensure that risks are promptly identified. 61. Plan for potential risks in the future.
Review and Improvement	62. Have a system in place to periodically review the efficiency of your legacy plan. 63. Seek the help of consultants or experts as needed. 64. Establish benchmarks and standards for optimal performance. 65. Prepare resources needed for the review and improvement process as well as the implementation of required changes. 66. Develop a culture of operational excellence and legacy optimization in your organization.

As shown in Table 10.4, there is a lot of intentionality and energy required in the process of legacy planning. A major reason why many individuals have not carried out their legacy plans is that they thought of it, but never acted on it. Some may not know how to implement it. The action agenda outlined in Table 10.4 shows practical steps you can take to implement your legacy plan in an efficient manner.

Art courtesy of Allison Brannon

CHAPTER 11

Concluding Thoughts

Please think about your legacy because you are writing it every day.
—Gary Vaynerchuk

The stories in this book highlight the fact that there are at least eight legacy pathways. There are many other ideas one can use to enrich legacy in a lifetime and truly make a lasting difference in the world.

In an article on legacy and impact, Eric Lau (2015), senior faculty at Leaderonomics, highlighted important legacy considerations such as looking into one's heart to make a difference, leveraging one's talent, using a circle of influence to find change, and not making money the end game.

George Raveling (2016), former head basketball coach of Washington State, Iowa, and USC offered several pointers to a meaningful legacy including: (1) serve rather than be served, (2) build on your strengths, (3) seek excellence, (4) show the world something new, (5) strengthen relationships, (6) prioritize your actions, (7) add value to other people's lives, (8) steer away from your comfort zone, (9) be a role model, and (10) help others achieve more than they think they can.

A life transition expert Bart Astor (2013) suggested the following: (1) creating a family history, (2) giving to charity, (3) crafting a legacy letter, and (4) putting together an ethical will.

Aspiriant Director in Wealth Management Gregory Fasig (2018) underscored the importance of (1) identifying what your legacy is, (2) sharing your desired legacy with others, (3) tying in your legacy into your daily life and activities, (4) gathering support for your legacy, (5) growing your legacy by educating others and leveraging your network, and (6) celebrating your legacy by bringing people together and sharing your progress.

Co-founder of the L Group, Lee Colan (2018) proposed sharing what you can in terms of time, treasure, and talent.

Author Larry Smith (2008) recommended the use of a six-word memoir to crystallize one's idea in terms of life's meaning and legacy.

I would further suggest the use of a model I call the **Legacy Diamond**—a three-angled action plan comprising of: (1) **Notion**—the idea or concept driving your legacy plan, (2) **Ambition**—the energy and drive that leads to a High Memory Capacity pursuit, and (3) **Execution**—the planning and implementation framework that transforms one's sense of purpose from dream to reality.

Figure 11.1 is an illustration of the **Legacy Diamond**.

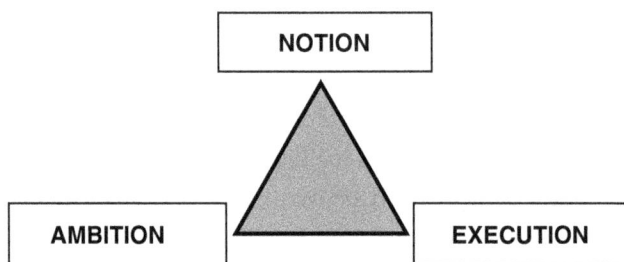

Figure 11.1 The legacy diamond

Table 11.1 shows a few examples of how the **Legacy Diamond** model may be utilized.

The **Legacy Diamond** underscores the fact that we must not just think and plan about legacy. In order to make a real impact, we need to take action and execute it. A successful legacy is the convergence of our true purpose, our desires, and our ability and intent of executing our plans.

As we approach the end of our lives, we all want to feel that we have made a difference. We all want to feel we've accomplished a goal and purpose and made this world better than when we first found it. This strong drive for fulfillment and purpose is what leads to the creation of nonprofit organizations, social enterprises, and philanthropic work all over the world.

For example, a Scottish-American businessman Andrew Carnegie donated money to build 2,509 Carnegie libraries across several countries. Nowadays, we see billionaires and millionaires passing on their wealth to charitable causes. In academia, we see wealthy patrons donating money

Table 11.1 Application of the legacy diamond

Person	Notion	Ambition	Execution
Student	Leverage social media marketing skills to create a lasting legacy	Driven and passionate about promoting entrepreneurship among minority youth	Use of the Strategic Legacy Plan model while aligning notion and ambition in the process of implementation *(Impact: Thousands of youth helped through minority entrepreneurship programs)*
Executive	Leverage supply chain and logistics skills to create a lasting legacy	Driven and passionate about the speedy assistance of victims in calamities and natural disasters	Use of the Strategic Legacy Plan model while aligning notion and ambition in the process of implementation *(Impact: Thousands of victims helped as a result to prompt emergency response programs worldwide)*
Retiree	Leverage excess financial resources to create a lasting legacy	Driven and passionate about the natural environment and its preservation worldwide	Use of the Strategic Legacy Plan model while aligning notion and ambition in the process of implementation *(Impact: Preservation of forests in several locations around the world)*

to have a building, stadium, or a school named in their honor. We see the elderly offering their services and donating money to the church. These acts of kindness were driven by a desire to make a significant difference and to enrich one's final legacy.

In the end, we leave behind fragments of our thoughts, ideas, values, deeds, and possessions. Most importantly, we leave behind our love—to our family, friends, and society. We leave behind our legacy of love, friendship, and community that accompanies our life story.

While the scope, scale, and depth of our legacies are important, it is the seemingly *small seeds of goodness* every day that adds to our legacies and shapes our personal stories. Creating a legacy is rarely a one-time event; it is a series of small acts that is built over time.

How we existed in our lifetime has implications not only on our Memorial Capacity but also our lingering impact on people and society. Your intellectual contributions by way of ideas would spur the creation of other ideas. The message of love you taught your loved ones will in turn define the way they love others in their own lifetime. Your charitable contributions would change the lives of several individuals and would in turn enable them to help others. One's legacy pays itself forward.

Ultimately, the way we live our lives define our story and legacy.

How will your son or daughter remember you? What about your grandchildren and great grandchildren? What about your spouse? Or your friends? The reality is that your personal legacy does not have to be grand. You have the ability to demonstrate the eight types of legacy to your loved ones in your own way—financial, social, political, intellectual, spiritual, cultural, physical, and historical. For instance, passing along money and possessions to loved ones will be some form of financial legacy. Taking your family on a foreign trip will be some form of cultural legacy. Teaching your children and grandchildren how to pray will be some form of spiritual legacy.

We are all empowered to create our legacies—simple or grand—in our own special way.

A conscious and dedicated effort toward this end will lead to more meaningful results. Our chosen courses of action will determine the future trajectory of our legacy and the impact it produces in years to come.

Bronnie Ware (2019), an Australian palliative nurse and author of the book, *The Five Regrets of the Dying,* underscored five actions those dying wished they had done differently: (1) allow oneself to be happier, (2) didn't work so hard, (3) courage to live a life true to oneself, (4) expressed real feelings, and (5) kept in touch with friends. When pursuing activities in line with your real purpose and happiness, you'll find your life to be of meaning and value. Consequently, you will be well poised to create and leave behind a powerful and lasting legacy.

How will you be remembered in 50 or more years? What type of Memorial Capacity will you have? How many lives have you impacted? Did you make the world a better place? The nuggets of wisdom from the stories and lessons in this book, the Strategic Legacy Plan (SLP) as well as the **Legacy Diamond**, could provide a roadmap to finding your true self and your discovery of meaningful and memorable pursuits along the way.

References

Astor, B. 2013. "4 Smart Ways to Leave a Legacy," *Forbes*. https://www.forbes.com/sites/nextavenue/2013/08/01/4-smart-ways-to-leave-a-legacy/#65823abd313c.

Colan, L. 2018. "How Leave a Legacy of Significance," *Inc*. https://www.inc.com/lee-colan/how-to-leave-a-legacy-of-significance.html.

Fasig, G. 2018. "6 Ways to Leaving an Impactful Legacy," *Aspiriant*. https://aspiriant.com/fathom/wealth-planning/6-steps-leaving-impactful-legacy/.

Lau, E. 2015. "Leaving a Legacy, Making an Impact," *Leaderonomics*. https://leaderonomics.com/leadership/leaving-a-legacy-making-an-impact.

Raveling, G. 2016. "21 Ways to Build a Meaningful Legacy," *Observer*. https://observer.com/2016/07/21-ways-to-build-a-meaningful-legacy/.

Smith, L. 2008. *One Life, 6 words—What's Yours?: Six-word Memoirs from Smith Magazine*. New York, NY: Harper Press.

Ware, B. 2019. *The Five Regrets of the Dying: A Life Transformed by the Dearly Departing*. Carlsbad, CA: Hay House.

Art courtesy of Allison Brannon

About the Author

J. Mark Munoz is a professor of management at Millikin University and former visiting fellow at the Kennedy School of Government at Harvard University. He is a recipient of several awards including four Best Research Paper Awards, two international book awards, a literary award, and the ACBSP Teaching Excellence Award, among others. Aside from top-tier journal publications, he has authored/edited/coedited more than 20 books in management and economics such as *International Social Entrepreneurship and Managerial Forensics*. As chairman/CEO of the international management consulting firm Munoz and Associates International, he directs and manages consulting projects for companies worldwide.

Index

OTHER TITLES IN BUSINESS CAREER DEVELOPMENT COLLECTION

Vilma Barr, *Editor*

- *Innovative Selling: A Guide to Successful Corporate Professional Selling* by Eden White
- *Present! Connect!: A Guide to Creating and Delivering Presentations That Capture, Entertain, and Connect to Any Audience* by Tom Guggino
- *Introduction to Business: A Primer On Basic Business Operations* by Patrice Flynn
- *Be Different!: The Key to Business and Career Success* by Stanley W. Silverman
- *Strategic Bootstrapping* by Matthew W. Rutherford
- *Financing New Ventures: An Entrepreneur's Guide to Business Angel Investment* by Geoffrey Gregson

Announcing the Business Expert Press Digital Library

Concise e-books business students need for classroom and research

This book can also be purchased in an e-book collection by your library as

- *a one-time purchase,*
- *that is owned forever,*
- *allows for simultaneous readers,*
- *has no restrictions on printing, and*
- *can be downloaded as PDFs from within the library community.*

Our digital library collections are a great solution to beat the rising cost of textbooks. E-books can be loaded into their course management systems or onto students' e-book readers. The **Business Expert Press** digital libraries are very affordable, with no obligation to buy in future years. For more information, please visit **www.businessexpertpress.com/librarians**. To set up a trial in the United States, please email **sales@businessexpertpress.com**.

www.ingramcontent.com/pod-product-compliance
Lightning Source LLC
Chambersburg PA
CBHW061839220326
41599CB00027B/5335